**VISIBLE
CITIES**

 **UNIVERSITY OF CALGARY** Press

# VISIBLE CITIES

*Kathleen Wall &*
*Veronica Geminder*

Brave & Brilliant Series
ISSN 2371-7238 (Print) ISSN 2371-7246 (Online)

© 2018 Kathleen Wall and Veronica Geminder

University of Calgary Press
2500 University Drive NW
Calgary, Alberta
Canada T2N 1N4

press.ucalgary.ca

This book is available as an ebook. The publisher should be contacted for any use which falls outside the terms of that license.

LIBRARY AND ARCHIVES CANADA CATALOGUING IN PUBLICATION

Wall, Kathleen, 1950-, author
    Visible cities / Kathleen Wall & Veronica Geminder.

(Brave & brilliant series, ISSN 2371-7238 ; 5)
Poems.
Issued in print and electronic formats.
ISBN 978-1-55238-959-1 (softcover).—ISBN 978-1-55238-960-7 (PDF).—
ISBN 978-1-55238-961-4 (EPUB).—ISBN 978-1-55238-962-1 (Kindle)

    1. Cities and towns—Poetry. 2. City and town life—Poetry. 3. Cities and towns—Pictorial works. 4. City and town life—Pictorial works. 5. Poetry. I. Geminder, Veronica, photographer II. Title. III. Series: Brave & brilliant series ; 5

PS8595.A5645V57 2018            C811'.54            C2017-907860-7

                                                                               C2017-907861-5

The University of Calgary Press acknowledges the support of the Government of Alberta through the Alberta Media Fund for our publications. We acknowledge the financial support of the Government of Canada. We acknowledge the financial support of the Canada Council for the Arts for our publishing program

Editing by Helen Hajnoczky
Cover image: Veronica Geminder, *University Bridge*, 2012, photograph
Cover design, page design, and typesetting by Melina Cusano

*For Ken Probert*

# I
## Beauty Unforeseen

Unforeseen | *3*
Quiet city | *7*
Rust à la Pollock | *11*
Rothko's wooden door | *15*
Maps | *19*
Curtains and wire | *23*
Your mind under glass | *27*

# II
## Questions in Our Pockets

Questions in our pockets | *33*
De Chirico on Wall Street | *39*
Haversack | *43*
Improvisation | *47*
Talking about the dogs | *51*
Margins | *55*
Dare | *59*
Ladders | *63*

# III
## What Would Banksy Do?

Street history | *67*
Graffiti | *71*
First snow | *75*
University Bridge | *79*
Yarn bombing in Grand Cerf Arcade | *83*

## IV
### Reflections in a Camera's Eye

Cloud Gate | *87*
Man in the blue shirt | *91*
Campus in the off hours | *95*
Red truck | *99*
Restore | *103*
Dance of chairs | *107*
Flea market | *111*
Orchids in Grand Cerf Arcade | *115*
Rue St. Honoré | *119*
Convex travel mirror | *121*

## V
### Grids

Daedalus at work | *125*
Threshold | *129*
Open | *131*
Reverie | *135*
The Chicago Picasso | *139*
Rue Descartes | *143*

Acknowledgements | *145*
Notes | *149*
Biographies | *151*

# I
## Beauty Unforeseen

# Unforeseen
*Ottawa*


In our cell phones we hoard
the instant of a skater's
arabesque, or that sunset we caught
two weeks ago between strip malls on the way
to buy two steaks and a bag of apples.
                                                  Yet

we fail to shelter the fleet-footedness
of beauty, its hoof prints leading
back into memory's grove, stopping
suddenly, no antelope nearby, leaving
discretion behind, like a Chagall goat.

Beauty is shy and rare, has tender
and mutable hiding places.
      Like that back lane

we pass every morning, late,
distracted.
     Giving attention we might catch
the architect's gesture toward serene geometry,
her love of a surface not glass, light
feathered in the blue shadow
of winter afternoons. Concrete
pelt of a blue goat.

The architect links one beauty
into another, glass and façade
with back lane in quiet courtesy:
the turbulence of brick
ruffling moleskin,

inviting a game of basketball.
As the players stride and strive,
their movements trace shadows on stark walls:
flickering shores, waves, crescent moons
described by swallows,
threaded on a blue story.

# Quiet city
*Chicago*

Loading dock with the patina
of smog, ceiled by wind, layered
with the yearly coat of paint, crowded
by dark impervious steel and glass.
Over-turned bin left by the caretaker
where he waits for a delivery and smokes
a private cigarette.

The back door of your life
is as starkly, lawlessly
eloquent, a plain-spoken relic
of the day you went home to wait
for the grey chairs to be delivered.

Lightning had cut the power
and all you could read in the late
afternoon dark was your cell phone.
You wanted something
sublime. You found Cheever's stories
and the wildflower guide. Instead
you watched the clouds billow
and unravel in the sharp blows of light.

You smoothed the weave of the tablecloth
and the weave of the afternoon
with words to teach simplicity
to time and storm.
A cold cup of coffee
rested on the table by the window,
thunder rippling in its liquid oval.

# Rust à la Pollock
*Saskatoon*

I
He pins the canvas to the floor, readying it
for gravity, for the chaos that drips and loops
through the unruly day: a muddled argument,
the unfixed kitchen tap, the one holy moment
when the day's breath gathers his attention
and the lightning illuminates that gash
into the other world where everything
means only itself.

He pins the canvas to the floor, wrestling
with the hurricane gravity of black and white.
Rust and yellow thrum among black filaments.
Materiality spills from his paint stick
in a spare lichen of thought.

Time circles with Pollock on the canvas.

II
What needs effacing behind a Chinese restaurant
in a back alley, making time and physics
ghosts? Rust and scratches become
a second in a calligraphic history
the photographer records.

Leaning his shoulder against the wall, he waits
for his girlfriend, a curvy waitress
dead on her feet. It doesn't matter. All he wants
is a fuck and a good night's sleep. He engraves
impatience in gashes on a parking sign.
He is a cliché—the pose, the lust—
yet his waiting oxidizes moments
dropping through rain and snow,
gusting into an alley one street over,
leaving a rusty diagram
of another galaxy.

So time and physics aren't ghosts
but the artists of chance and change.
                              How much beauty
is wrought by wind and rain? Antique maps
traced on camellia petals. Pollock abstracts among
trees and time torn up by the roots.  How many
layers of subplot and chronicle
have been erased or rediscovered by a scraping key
or nail file? Destruction also
is mysterious.

# Rothko's wooden door
*Saskatoon*

What does an art student know
about business, except maybe
the difference between what's good
and what sells? The insurance guy
comes and says the back door is all
wrong.
    *The sidelight breaks in two seconds
and the perp reaches in and unlocks your
deadbolt in a wink. Also, don't put your
name on the door back here: keep 'em
guessing.*
                  He's looked at my prices
but hasn't thought about why someone
hungry for high or oblivion would think
he could hawk a Benjamin Chee Chee repro
or an owl by Josie Iqaluk
on a Saskatoon street corner.

So when my dad still knew
what tools were for, he hammered
plywood over the sidelight. I painted
a rough square of blue, just
over the name—Amberly & Sons—
raising whorls like watered silk while it dried.
Rothko knew how little we need
to make a door: layers of thin paint
mingling, dissolving inside and out.
The back lane's layers
of paper and paint are accidental keepers
of time, fading and splitting in sun and rain.

When I visit my father now I tell
stories with no threads dangling
in the past, or any characters
he'll have forgotten. I use
simple words like *window* or *glass*—
something he sees in his room.

# Maps
*Ottawa*

*Wow! That's a sketchy*
*alley* says the dude in front
of us to his girlfriend
whose stilettos echo
along the street. He carries
his after-dinner/pre-game
twelve-pack, the bottles
clinking in time
to the flash
of her hoop earrings
along Lord Elgin's
Tyndall stone walls. While

three young women round the corner
in front of him, swinging down the alley
in unison, a stream of stars from a spangled
nebula in a blue retreat from the telescope.
One quickly checks her cell phone
while their skirts sway and shift like auroras.
They took no unexpected detour
suggested by one curious woman.
This is their chosen route. We all

have our secret maps, knowing
where the noon traffic gets heavy,
circumnavigating spring puddles,
calculating the shortest, quickest route,
often on the back streets. Just so
these three women choose to carve
their own city.

# Curtains and wire
*Saskatoon*

The curtain, yes,
well, this is where I fetched up, like foam
on a beach or elm seeds in a storm drain. Or a bear
in a cage it stumbled on in the woods, waiting
for that noisy moving dizzying thing
to stop, waiting for earth on my paws or earth
in my fur. It's what happens
when you do something impulsive,
like getting on the first bus

and finding out where you're going afterwards. Maybe
it was the wind smelling of wormwood,
bitter, antiseptic, scouring. Or the way the clouds
lined up on the horizon like breakers on a beach:
I couldn't face the undertow. Maybe it was a word:
like *beginning*, or *desert*, or *anarchy*.

Or the way the mute cold ate words. This was all
I could find downtown, window on a back alley.
So the curtain says *sanctuary, lair*; it says
the smell of bleach and the order of ironing.
The wires say *risk, hazard*.
I like where the shadows meet.

# Your mind under glass
*Chicago*

This might be your mind
with its brick facts
built up one by one,
from hunger to calculus,
from the slipperiness of sex
and the stock market
to the day you began
Act III, the day the alarm
didn't go off
and you learned
what it means to stretch
into mortal thoughts—how
joyous and how grave!

You might want to question
the windows: do you look in
at privacy and nakedness,
at secret desires, rogue ideas;
or out toward weather, scandal,
power-plays? You keep taking
expected routes to avoid climbing
down the fire-escapes
to wrestle with wisdom.

But the black paint is thick,
scarred with use, rough
on your hands. You catch a whiff
of the alley and often decide
you don't want to jump that far.

What you don't see each day
is how green it is.
There's a tower you keep
trying to climb.
But you're out of shape.
It diffuses light everywhere
in shadows and highlights. Much
of the world comes to you here,
longing for a little face time,
confused
by the glass, drawn
by the open stairway.

Some days you baulk
at the idea that everything
your mind has turned over
has purpose. You await
some ordinary event
that will illuminate the universe
like the afternoon sun
blazoning a handful of bricks,
marking the edge
of something you'd forgotten—
exactly what will measure
or enclose your life
like a frame.

## II
## Questions in Our Pockets

Behind the cotton wool is hidden a pattern; that we—I mean all human beings—are connected with this; that the whole world is a work of art; that we are parts of the work of art. Hamlet or a Beethoven quartet is the truth about this vast mass that we call the world. But there is no Shakespeare, there is no Beethoven; certainly and emphatically there is no God; we are the words; we are the music; we are the thing itself.

—Virginia Woolf, *Moments of Being*

# Questions in our pockets
*Boston Common*

I
The moment is never simple. When
you choose the flattest stones and skip them
four times into oncoming waves. When
you read, and looking up see your book
alive in the afternoon, its pages
unbound, spread in the dark
clematis purple of the world. When
you are as skillful with a shovel and a word
as with a saucepan and a song. When
you walk down an unlit hallway in the frail shadows
of November afternoons to look for windows. When
you choose the flattest stones. When
the throat of the lily breathes in light, when
the book unbinds. Then
you plant your feet in the memory
loam of this moment as deeply
as a tree in time and weather, then

you want someone to take your picture.

II
*… so he gnawed his neighbour's balls off,*
Antonio Cassese, Bosnian war crimes judge,
tells the journalist, simply.

          Lunchtime,
Cassese goes to The Hague's Vermeers.
The painter casts a transient light on the moment
of measured courage to be oneself,
to begin to turn one's head, pour milk,
or play the lute, as if it were ordinary
to find the span
between one thing and the next.

      (Just as you hope someone takes
      a picture of you comprehending
      a lover or a friend,
      a portrait of you listening for that plod of grief
      in her voice you heard last week, as you studied
      the shadow that does not disappear at noon but radiates
      from her hands like a bracelet or a blessing.)

The model's thought immaterial and imaged, unplumbed,
free.

III
One hundred twenty years too late, these people
gathered on Boston Common sit
for Seurat's *A Sunday Afternoon on the Island
of La Grande Jatte*. Though here,
there are lovers: he pets the dog, wondering how
the dog keeps its composure or finds
excitement in the daily round.
She stares into the blinding sunlight of an argument.

But always, there is the girl in the water just
turning toward all the visible and invisible
questions, to stare them down before she puts them,
like stones, in her damp pocket.

IV
Just as there is always a girl, so
there is also an old woman
watching the girl. Knowing
she is invisible to painter or photographer,
this afternoon she paints for herself
one of her many portraits.

"Decades ago, my lover
said my eyes were like green stones.
The simile spread like lava:
heart, womb. When his girlfriend
and baby fetched up at the door
needing money for formula,
I gave them his jar of change
and my key, pulled his suitcase
from under the bed, packed
and left.

"There, on the street, I saw the office girl
and the whore, the crone
with ivory hands and a knowing gleam,
a balletic girl tracing the edge
of the fountain with slender pointed feet,
a little girl in a swing wild
for underducks.

"Looking at me now, who knows the stone,
small, round, heavier than gravity, lodged
beside a radiance still roused by small
adventures—cinnamon, saucy questions,
Mary Pratt's white sheets
in a crimson bed—begetting a woman, loose, an aficionado
of misrule, artlessness, and triumph, a woman hungry
for anarchic music.

"There. I see her called out of her damp
daydream, dragging her feet until the dog
joins her. She makes for herself a moment
she will remember when she is my age:
a straight, strong spine, a pirouette,
one hand slapping the sun because
she knows the painter stands somewhere
so that what memory forgets art will remember."

## De Chirico on Wall Street
*New York City Financial District*

If a coin fell here,
its echo would ring
down the loggia and ricochet
from brick to glass.
Then the silence of the street,
the order of the columns
and squared ceilings,
would muffle its stop on the brick.

What could you set
between the columns
or under the lights
that would not need its echo?
A cowbird's egg.
A trundling hoop.
An architect's model of a skyscraper
swaying in the Japanese earthquake,
its glass singing.

The shadowed proportions of the loggia
should tell stories about the women
who make an alley their own.
Or about your long walk on a winter road
at midday, when the power
was out, thick hoarfrost
falling from the trees in chunks,
your glove clasping your wife's cold hand,
your eyes on the slick path.

Learning to live here means admiring
the order of midafternoons that empty
like de Chirico's melancholy streets,
pursuing indifferent beauty.

Place an egg there,
a hoop, the model
of a skyscraper, see
who will trip,
what echoes.

# Haversack
*New York City*

This morning the wind was up, keening
between the high rises. Brushing the crumbs
off the newspaper, he read about a boxing match,
the Yankees in Tampa, even glanced at full-page fashion ads.
He wrote a cheque, sealed it in an envelope with his key,
sat back to take another swallow of his cooling coffee,

and looked up.
In this weather, with the wind and the Hudson
scuffled green he wants to find
*away*, that quiet place with no echoes,
no phone numbers or dates pencilled on the walls
near the empty phone, to find the hollow shell
where the day's light, moving across a room, doesn't blazon
leftover posters: a Picasso bouquet
changing hands, a small curling botanical

with flurried rows of eggs. Scraps
from other people's lives keep falling into his with their ache:
two bobby pins swept up on Saturday, a bottle of blue pills
finally jostled to the front of the silverware drawer.
In his mailbox, a scented letter to Sam, a postcard of a melting
Gaudí home whose message is a second address.

There's not much here he wants. His socks. Jockeys.
Spare jeans and shirt. A sweater.
Laptop. No cell phone. He knows
stripping down to need has an integrity
and lightness he can't convince his booted feet to feel.

This is a common emergence, those days
when you turn your back and do not
believe in doorways. The exit you take,
without sympathy or questions, in a blind
panic, when you throw up your arm
to protect your face or widen
the path through the undergrowth.

# Improvisation
*New York City*


His walk has the canter
of confidence, a shoulder bravado
that fills the space he weaves between nannies
and men with briefcases, giving wide berth
to a pair of fervent young men in yarmulkes
carrying posters, pamphlets, and a table,
and arguing definitions: *It depends
on what you mean…*
by something like the ethics
of taking doctrine into the green
and rebellious morning
of Washington Square. He gravitates
to the southern chess district,
but on his way he shows
how each day our minds reach out
with a surprised hand,

an enclosing arm,
a turning ankle to improvise
our easy segue around the fountain,
how in Washington Square we dance
with an invisible partner
or one unknown twelve feet away, tied to us
by the rhythms of space.

Arriving at the chess board, his mind
is already at play, fingers
tickling strategies, imagining the next
move. He dreams the unbeatable player

he can defeat, the window
to a fresh play not in the books. He tastes
the metallic cleft between winning and losing.
Yet he leaves the door ajar to glimpse
his opponent's eyes, the way the irises flare
and settle, the laconic conversation these players
pretend not to make but use like a password
to say everything important about the improvisations
in Washington Square, the shadow music that floats
through the six directions they might choose.

# Talking about the dogs
*Chicago*

If I look up, I see you smirk, assuming
that we, like your parents,
have nothing left
to talk about but the dogs. You presume
at best we're still agile enough
now and then to dance around
landmines that explode exactly
the way they have for years;
or that, Houdini-like, we escape conversations
naked with boredom. You're wondering
if one of us has lost his hearing
or the muscle's memories marking
the way to the right house.
You want proof:

for me or you? Here it is.
This morning I trimmed back the mock orange,
those needle shoots that bear the flower then
turn the bush to a spiny creature
I tame. So each late spring
I'm summoned to memory: the backache
of putting in the garden, new daughter
dozing in the umbroller, the cold
of unneeded milk leaking from taut breasts.

And then next year, a snapshot of my girl
standing next to my stretching plants,
my alarming shadow over the whole noticed
only when the prints came back.

In your young mockery, how do you know
we're not talking in code about
the questions that now descend
noiselessly into each day?
Does the dog have a Buddha nature?
Do we? Or maybe the curling fur
we pluck at with dry querying fingers
is our symbol for the apple trees in our first
back yard, blooming in ecstasy but setting
little fruit. Or a metaphor
for the cloudy days that spoiled our first
vacation but taught us
to play double Solitaire
and laugh at our furious rivalry, as if
we'd decided (without deciding)
that the victor rode the loser
into paradise 'til the loons went silent.

What you don't know is how we seek
this space just beneath the street
to sit near the begonias, how its quilt
of air and words and faces
frees us into stories. I hear silverware
and china clink patiently behind me
where I earlier heard an abstract conversation
about paint—just words like *teal* or *taupe*
or *bluegreygreen*. And *love* or *no*.
                              It was like glimpsing
a living room at dusk on an evening walk
and feeling the silhouette of a conversation
embodied everything that went on in that house, so potently
the gestures stood out against the light.
                              From under the stairs
come the rowdy chants of girls
running and hiding and making a secret space
for their secret selves.

We're not through with stories, though sometimes,
like good Buddhists of the everyday,
we do talk about the dogs.

# Margins
*Chicago*

When we're seven we hang
around borders, edge one-
eyed around
corners, play
hide and seek
everywhere, disguised
watchers studying
arguments, punishments
and all their consequences
for our own rebellions.

We create rituals anointing
the play our parents
censure, playing doctor
or giving secret absolution
in spaces small enough
to be confessionals.

We gather intel on the adults
while laughing
at their lack of disguise.

We play with light and dark,
seen and unseen,
throwing them ever higher
over our heads to see
how high they can go
before they fall
through our hands. Then
we study what happens.

We are joyfully
relentless.

# Dare
*New York City*

Three boys swarm the band shell
with skateboards and nerve. Forget
the neoclassical frieze, the arch that holds
Gershwin and Handel in its head
on summer nights between silent
invisible stars. These ramps and steps
launch boys toward a future so airborne
they forget gravity and duty. The acoustics
are perfect to let challenge

    *Betcha can't!*
and success
     *Hey! Lookit this!*
skirl into the park.

     Nearby,
on The Mall, a roller skater
swoops and swirls to the music
on her Walkman, her venerable skates (no
in-line cheats for her) and 'tude rescued
from adolescence. No modest pose,
no female urge to study
her hands and feet, to sing
under her breath.

She opens her arms wide
to the beneficent gods
of balance
        and an audience
that doesn't matter, sings tunelessly
at the top of her voice to music
we can't hear. Her in-turned eyes
and out-turned skin—a rendezvous.

We crave this theatre
on Sunday afternoons
when we dare who we are.

# Ladders
*Regina*

Even near the skyline: grids
and turbines drive
sunlit air down to the first storey
while drowning out
the relentless coo and whir of pigeons
who edge the colourless grey
of these plain-spoken horizontals.

As you strain against physics—
fulcrums and friction—
how can you have forgotten your bucket
of tools and all you knew
about putting up clean storm windows
or showing your daughter fireworks
from the balcony?
                        Truth is
we all pull our escape routes up
behind us sometimes and flatten
our lives to maps.

No one can come up. You are
Rapunzel in a ball cap. What
will you do with such airy
solitude in your concrete eyrie?
Play endless games of Solitaire
and recalculate your odds?
Read Proust straight through?
You could thicken the skin
your last divorce scrubbed away
or get over shyness by parsing its limits.

But you also can't get out. When 2 a.m.
comes round, you can't roam
downstairs with the excuse of wanting
a glass of water or craving
yesterday's leftovers. There's no reason
for parting the kitchen curtain to see
if the voices you hear belong to strangers
uprooting the neighbour's garden.

# III
## What Would Banksy Do?

You get inside people's heads and vandalize their eyeballs.

—Don DeLillo, *Underworld*

# Street history
*Ottawa*

Here's where we bring the indoors out, confess
our carelessness about the dog, plans to crochet
flowers up and down the no parking signs
of the neighbourhood, maybe even
yarn bomb a bus or two. Here's where we sing
that someone's cat came back and could the owner
please call?

Here's our neighbourhood speaker's corner
where we flog the latest magic show,
the requiem mass we'll sing, the cowboy
poetry reading, advice on choosing shrubs
for shade.

Our hand-made signs for the garage sale,
outlined letters launched into life by children
with markers, will run when it rains tomorrow.
So we wrap them in plastic, trying to mummify today:
the smell of our daughters' hair and the tang
of markers mingling with the gritty nose of sand.

This is our history, its illegible fragments
interrupting one another, the accident
of the lost cat vying with the well-rehearsed
all candidates' forum. Here hot-coloured,
passionate shouts of the proselytizer drain
to black and white. Push pins quarrel
with staples about longevity. The estate sale
marks the dispersal of history's seeds
to other homes, out of context:
visible, obscure.

# Graffiti
*Railroad siding between Regina and Saskatoon*

First the doodle of it: old
pencil crayons still smelling
of school, slightly chewed. This
is not the portrait of Ed M
that looked like a tame van Gogh.
Here you create
the technicolor language
of your cynicism or joyful
rebellion as it passes each
crossing where the lined-up
cars wait and wait. Then

rehearsals. Drafts.
You sketch
fonts on basement walls
and seek words
eager to morph,
like the Mediaeval monk's capitals,
until the world of your voice
grows inside each letter.

Done in anger, defiance. In praise.
To record. To forget. To vandalize
eyeballs. Take back space. Then

scale. You've walked the length
of a car between its wheels
in the rail yards north of downtown, roughly
guessed the distance. Then
the paint, the night, the physics
of body and art: the aluminum pock
of the metal ball, the hiss of 3D, of outlining,
shading, highlights, baroque wildstyle arrows,
your words and world
exploding somewhere different
every day
into the dawn.

# First snow
*Regina*

Sometimes, more than a little drunk
after a friendly dinner, talkative,
candles and sated minds down to their pulse,
we idly ask *How did we come to talk
about childhood dreams of burning houses,
the half dozen guiding words from a poem
we've otherwise forgotten, the shapes
of hooves and padded feet we've scribbled
on a napkin?* Sometimes we trace ourselves
back, more often giving up in laughter
and moving to the next room to sit—
for a moment, each of us alone—
by the fire.

Just so, we emerge from conversations, spending
sprees and midlife crises confused, eavesdroppers
on our own lives, with neither energy nor curiosity
to unravel back to beginnings, our paths
labyrinths for geniuses or cheerful fools. One

luminous day: an early snow, the parking lot
a calligrapher's page. Coming from work that needs
the antidote of Crosby, Stills, and Nash—
usually music for the first spring day—we're singing how
*We never failed to fail; it was the easiest thing to do*
and trying to name the flame-shaped trees.

*She is all that I have left and music is her name,*
we sing, thick-throated, as we turn on the heat for the first time
this winter and consider the riches of having
only music. Simple changes do this, clear the air
for a shot of perspective. Reversing, we see
where we've been, but the laneway

is blocked and music has made us mellow. Suddenly
the pigeons swerve above the snow, furling
and unfurling early winter white and grey. Looking back
we see the arc of our tracks, the shape
we have just made.

# University Bridge
*Saskatoon*

A lecture at the gallery—
*The Influences of Neolithic Architecture,
Particularly Dolmens and Menhirs,
on Contemporary Monumental Painting*—
one of those late afternoon events attended
by four and a half people. You've seen her
at other lectures or concerts—
both of you "getting out" as your friends insist:
your shy version of online dating. What
was there to say about Neolithic architecture
in the Japanese Garden?
You hesitated at the irresistible green
of a maple on the edge of russet, briefly
studied the heavy, earthbound lantern.

You both walked, a sign of—
something, and so fell in step along the river.
Spring made the green conversation,
thin as a new, unfolded leaf,
brush the edge of wit. Until
you walked under University Bridge,
stopped abruptly by the sound of the full river
and reflected light dancing on concrete.

*Dolmen or menhir?* she asked, these
words rippling through the day.
*Not with those archways. I know kids
who climb the arches to the floor of the bridge
for bragging rights to a little athletic graffiti.*
She demurred. *If you look straight ahead—
ignore the arches—look into the distance.
All those long verticals
topped by monumental horizons?"*
You are about to say *No burials under swift water* when
you stop yourself, try to see what she sees.

You are just far enough from breakup
to be in love with loneliness. It's the urge to see
as someone else does, with its wry prod,
like a sharp iris leaf emerging from cool soil,
that makes you want to stand where she is standing.
*How about a suite of rooms enfilade?* she asks,
explaining the long path of endless, rhythmic
doorways, the courtly progress, the temptation
to run the length. You look again.
The river runs between the pilings. There is
no path.

*We could thread them on a kite, on the*
*string of one of Banksy's red balloons,*
*the little girl just there*, you point,
*at the high water mark.*

# Yarn bombing in Grand Cerf Arcade
*Paris*

You take your bearings.
From the wrought iron gates of Grand Cerf Arcade
you turn back to see *Sex Shop* in blue neon;
*Sex Center* in red, both in English promising
*video projection*. Across the way, in Passage du Bourg L'Abbé,
you read graffiti like the window menus
of respectable cafés—Le Pas Sage or Le Royal Bistro,
whose diners' eyes have that decent, urban Parisian gaze
that doesn't see what doesn't suit.

Inside, it's 1825 on the tessellated floors,
the old glass of the arcades two storeys high,
antiques and shiny crafts, Walter Benjamin eyeglasses
at Pour Vos Beaux Yeux. A woman
in a wedding dress outside La Corbeille,
(there's no room in the tiny shop)
her train trailing through the watery light:
a white mermaid. In Lil Weasel there are
no spinner's weasels, but a library of wool,

with its ladder. From time to time a naked
dress form observes Passage du Grand Cerf wearing
nothing but a lacy shawl or six cards of buttons
stamped with oak leaves or starfish, or run through
with pearled shawl pins, a Saint Sebastian
for knitters.

One winter in the early dark, four guerilla
knitters and a husband with long arms collect
to yarn bomb the arcade's gates with knitted
seaweed, coral, and anemones. What
do they think they're doing? Giving the lie
to the sex flicks with their own seductions
of beauty or plunging down the arcade's years
like a time tunnel to bring Atlantis back
to Paris with colours brighter than the sea's?
Their laughter shields them from bone-biting
November cold like a diving bell.

# IV
## Reflections in a Camera's Eye

# Cloud Gate
*Chicago*


Yes, it has its head in the clouds, clouds
on its mind, indifferently
contemplates the weather by day,
at night the blue toil of stars,
reminding us of someone cleaning
a house or writing a poem
and never finishing or forever walking off
into the wilderness. The skyline
encircles Cloud Gate, a corona
orbiting silver gravity.

That mercurial gate draws us into
the funhouse mirrors to take
pictures of ourselves taking
pictures of ourselves. If we dare
to witness the tangle of our thoughts,
we can pretend to laugh
under Cloud Gate's arch,
throwing our heads back, glancing
at the ceiling to catch the divine view.
But when we do, perspective morphs,

and what was close moves instantly farther
away: like a bird's wing or a finger
reaching out for ours: a greeting
we relinquish to the sudden distance.

                                              (Before bed
tonight, you will rehearse alone that
defensive photogenic smile you keep
in your pocket, to glimpse in a trick of light
nothing in the window behind you.)

# Man in the blue shirt
*Chicago*


This is your fantasy when you wait
for the red light, for the drycleaner's rack
to swing around to your ticket number,
for traffic jams and the end of your child's soccer game
when the evenings are still cold and soft rain
is almost coming down.

Subdued, on windless cloudy days, maybe
your sound track is Debussy chatting
with Monet, the two of them thinking
colour, thinking how subtly
greys and creams and mauves can shift
and tremble in Chicago fog. Maybe

in the rain, Moonalice tells you to "Dance
inside the Lightning." Maybe sunshine comes
with clapping hands and the vinyl scratch
of an old spiritual, the heat of fields, the intricate
smell of loam.

How, in your crisp blue shirt,
you will go back to the mahogany and silver office
after lunch, look out the dark glass at the street, down
at heads with their spectral thoughts.

And at the same time you will go to the market,
stand under a white canopy to buy
strawberries for your children's breakfast.
For your lover,
a handful of brilliant sunflowers
like wild gems, their seedy centre
growing with the mathematics of a crystal.
Thinking of gardeners and van Gogh,
you will stumble and brush
against Calder's red stabile and catch
a little red paint on your cuff.

# Campus in the off hours
*Regina*

Late on an autumn Friday: a sweet
desolation. The only ones left
are the loners who stare down group projects
and maybe class discussion, those who face
the stubborn book alone, those who know
the magic of mind
mingling with page, who love the smell
of textbook ink, turning pages
and ideas back and forth like a dancer
searching for a partner in the fourth dimension.

This is the hour when space and time disappear
into the vortex of curiosity, when you find the clew
to the labyrinth in a single word you know
by sight, but have never heard
out loud. In the glowing darkness
beyond your desk you compose new songs
from the rustle and crunch of dry leaves
and sing them under your breath.
Patterns of poetry and physics
are mapped over the tangle
of your synapses.

Nothing is where it is, or is
where it belongs. The table
where you sketch your premise stretches
beyond the glass, into the trees. Ideas
have gone outside, onto the Academic Green,
to stretch in the dark, then sit
at the table among the stones,
gossiping.

# Red truck
*Regina*

All the things that hold us up—
        staircases and porches,
        tremulous balconies hovering
        over terra firma, a bridge with a dead end—

All the things that hold up our minds—
        books and bookshelves
        carefully braced for the weights
        of words (some of the short words
        being heavier),
        that hold up our public selves—
        whalebone, suspenders and garters,
        that root us in space—
        handrails and architraves—

All the frames we set in place—
        windows and doors
        superstitions and philosophies,
        mantras to tame the frost
        that rimes across our window,
        but melts before we understand it—

—All this doesn't promise that the mirror won't crack
so that half the red truck with a stairway in its bed
falls out of place, and more sky
comes into being at the sound of breaking glass—

—Or that something puzzling—
is it a palm tree from a nearby pub,
or a gas line, as the dog walker argues?—
won't be left inert on the front porch of our days
for us to untangle one-handed
while we drink a glass of water,
note the accidental beauty of shadows
on curtains, walk onto the balcony
with a slice of still-warm bread.

# Restore
*Regina*

The photographer paces among
the dust motes, the old summer doors
with their wood and metallic clap
barely echoing among curtain rods
and oak banisters that have come
unmoored. She paces and waits
for the wind to sand the sun free
of clouds, for steady light that streams
an annunciation. When it comes
what she sees is how eyes and light

conspire to conjure radiance,
how the reflection of bricks
makes walls out of windows.
The moment the camera's shutter
flicks open is a meditation on the mystery
of vision: how even when we sleep
one eye opens inwardly,
how the thick green layers of glass
look like the sea's eyes studying stillness.

Blood was spilled in the blindings
of Gloucester and Argos,
blood assuaged by the family who studied
the green and gold prairie light
through these windows, read the pages of winter,
and before the house was left to weather,
lifted each pane carefully down to pile them here.

# Dance of chairs
*New York City*

Skyline, massive and fragile,
unsurprised light on a fresco of glass,
the city's grid an ornament grafted
above the aluminum skin
of weatherproof chairs and a table.

What could happen here?

Well, on the table there could be
two coffee mugs. His might be
stolid regulation white, only
slightly stained. Hers—
she'd have something handmade,
wouldn't she? With a divot of clay
on the handle inviting her thumb.
Between them, you might find
a fat paperback half read, in the middle
of the crisis, judging from the bookmark.

He'd be working on *The Times* crossword.
They might abandon both for a photograph
she holds: her white-haired father
dwarfed by the silvery glass
of a Wall Street office building.
His automatic smile faces forward,
his eyes anxiously turn to someone
on his left, a hand out as if for balance.

Seeing the photo, he imagines
the hours of care at the tired end of a day,
the stories behind every gesture
she makes: her arm flung up
in frustration, her flailing pen,
tentative hug. Yet music
tugs at her sleeve,
Bach, Mahler, Brubeck, Metheny
sings in her ready chortle.

Behind them, a man turns away
from his view of the Hudson
toward bleached thoughts of life or love,
something metaphysical
that explains how his eyes feel,
the emptiness behind them
when they're so full. He is
wizened and lean. Questions
wander slowly up his spine
like rime growing across a window.
He refuses to think
of the river, luminous green today,
with its small and brittle waves.

# Flea market
*Chicago*

Street markets invite
people brave enough
to flaunt their mania for tea
or trilby hats, for the alchemy
of polished stones or chrome. Or brave enough
to put memories on the street between
industrial walls that twinkle in the bowls
of silver spoons. Gravity goes missing
as tables sag and explode with vintage
linens. The thin mistress of minimal dress,

approving her lean lines, frowns impassively
as a model on a catwalk. A frowsty matron
bumps a table while she beetles toward her stall
to meet a customer. Plates rattle and collide
with salt and pepper shakers, Daffy Duck taking on
Jim Crow, watched by placid cows, applauded
by chickens: a lifetime of kitsch gone rogue.

Kitsch and thrift gone *dans la rue*.
Homeless teacups—flow blue, chipped,
minus saucers—wanting to go home.

At the market's centre: a man obsessed
with frames and geometry: tin ceiling tiles,
fences waiting for the suicide,
bed frames rusted into quaintness,
mirrors, mirrors, mirrors
where we glimpse ourselves,
freshen our lipstick or parse
the cut of our beards, faced
with industrial brickwork
and the spoils of clouds.

# Orchids in Grand Cerf Arcade
*Paris*

What dream is this? What palimpsest
of staircase, orchids, words,
and spectral reflections
from the shop across the arcade?

You have appeared in Proust's pages
in your plaid flannel nightgown,
and the socks you wear to bed in winter.
Fearing you'll slip on the narrow spiral staircase,

you take them off and watch them
dissolve into the checkered floor.
The palms of your hands yearn
to touch the ceiling medallions, but

your fingers need to stroke the waxy orchids,
certain their mute knowledge
will make up for all your failings
in dreams and waking.

But here's the catch: once you've
floated, grazing fingers
along ceiling volutes and mouldings,
down cool wrought iron, along the springing

stem of a perfect orchid growing
in a Paris arcade, you must step
backwards, down the staircase
into your own history.

# Rue St. Honoré
*Paris*

Strict or playful glass
geometries with tidy twentieth-
century angles are astonished

to be adorned with nineteenth-century
curly balconies and mansard roofs
built to Haussmann's specs.

Glass is so obliging about
inside and outside, so clearly
in love with ambiguity,

with the eyes' defiance
of here and there that leaves
the body behind.

Invisible or reflective, glass
has no heartwood to question
then and now, or to wonder how,

in the sublime caprice
with time, ghosts
hover.

# Convex travel mirror
*Venice*

At almost every bridge that spans
the Grand Canal, vendors sell selfie sticks
to the snatch-and-grab tourists
who flow through twisting
streets connecting San Marco
with Missoni. Other visitors take close-ups
of their mannered Venetian smiles
("I'm really here!") that blot out context:
no water, bridge, mosaics or piazzas.
Please stop to note
the frames ornate or graceful, gilded,
or of simply-turned wood
that might encircle, yes,
the masks and Murano glass clichés,
but also the thousand impressions
of San Marco that travelers unfold
under the wheeling gulls:

stories found carved on columns,
chaotic order of the Basilica.
Yes, so much of what you see
is yourself or your lonely ghost,
and there always is that gate or the bars
made by your baggage. But
you can stand pretending to study
the mirrors in the window
and see the reflected streets and shops
behind you, fragmentary,
wavering in the glass, distorted,
their foreignness just
within reach.

# V
## Grids

# Daedalus at work
*Ottawa*

First the frame. The trellis of cranes,
the lattices of iron unhinged
from sky, looking less like support
than ambition. Or is it longing? Between
the outlines of pillars, the wilderness
of work stopped mid-stride is disorder
resisting the dogma hidden
beneath office routine.

Beyond, glass boxes broadcast
weather reports in the warrens
that close in. We rely on their mirrors
to repeat and repeat our surroundings,
putting off the horizon.

In the midst of calls and texts and crowds
jostling and jarring for time
and space, they tell us where we stand.

Through the windows in the walls,
we watch how enterprise
grows faster than a tree or child, witness
the sorcery and honor of geometry.

We watch the art of silent bodies lifting
and pounding, fastening, carrying,
by plan and purpose driven,
but with no privacy
for stretched muscle or stiff spine,
this morning's ache or last night's
rapture. What happens to the questions
of swallow and waterfall, of mind
outside itself in fireworks or prayer?
Perhaps enigmas are scribbled or drawn
on beam or joist somewhere inside
this rigid thing rising on the street.

# Threshold
*Montreal*

First, the light.
Contemplative light I have seen
in a St. Germain side chapel hidden
from the Baroque.
And in a small Saskatchewan church
poised above a glacial gash,
windows focusing light
like the thick base of a jam jar.
Diffuse light in old libraries, glass
dating back to the time of Wren, etched
by industrial rain. Its soft radiance
falls on cracked leather chairs
and bindings softened by thought.

Then the threshold's embrace bursts
open to the street. Men in hard hats
cross and recross, putting out the sign
to remind St. Laurent shoppers *Trottoir Barré*.
Machinery rests in rubble, having hollowed
the building, plowing through pews and altar.

How do we enter mute space? Reason
needs words that traipse
in and out and in and out,
crossing and recrossing each time
a different threshold.

# Open
*New York City*

The respectable skyline: windows in a concrete grid, polite
crystals of light, uniform curtains joined in monologue

to close the conversation with the street, with traffic,
with the ecstasy of the museum-goer and the teens

coming from Fifth with autographed shopping bags
like bridles on thin wrists, joyful girls in platform

shoes with labyrinthine straps to keep them above
the streets. Uniform curtains drawn against the dark

that won't be silent, trucks making deliveries
at 5 a.m., insomniac street lights

never off till after dawn. Past angular columns
of parking by-laws stands

a ziggurat of graffiti-sprayed fire escapes,
as if the antidote to rules were curve and zig and

zag. Next door, all the secrets in the demolished building
have been peeled open before evaporating like a ghost's

frail perfume. The lime green comic
the 17-year-old boy drew along the baseboard,

lying on his belly, chin embossed by the shag,
the life of city streets drawn as Picasso drew Quixote:

angular and sharp. Panhandler and businessman,
art critic (long hair, black glasses) and model

argue about architecture and ugliness.
Drifting from the opened rooms are all the words

ever read here like *rapscallion* and *hope* and *wait*, the cereal
boxes read at breakfast and the newspapers at dinnertime.

Stories with heartbreaking plots, with heart-stopping
risk, the quiet dignity that sits still and listens

grips the neighbourhood. The floury warmth
of kneaded dough and the smell of bread,

the meal that makes frightened strangers smile
as they look through the lighted window and see

beyond the flimsy curtains the enigmatic tableau:
one leaning over the table—listening, threatening,

or simply stiff? In the taxi taking a shortcut
to 7th Ave, riders glimpse the boredom,

the freshness of human weather as we sit
with one another or stare into the street.

# Reverie
*Paris*

I
There are novels in some photographs—or we find them there as we move from figure to ground and back. We can imagine you needed to go out for a smoke—a respectable Parisian excuse. You lean into it, jaunty, rebellious, seeming at your ease, knowing the brick wall's got your back. Some days that Gallic jauntiness is pure spin. Your ad copy is coming slowly because you're also thinking about how you're going to have to work so fucking late. But you can't stay late because you've got to pick up your son at his school and take him home at the same time when really you should be chatting casually with your father-in-law whose dementia means he listens only to you and you're halfway to convincing him he'd like someone besides his wife to cook food he actually likes, someone else to argue with him (or not) about showers and shaving. You will not use the words *nursing home*. Meanwhile your wife is tired, but making dinner, and you imagine her wondering how much longer her mother can go on opening disgusting cans of smoked oysters and tinned pasta and plastic cups of pudding. Your father-in-law, who used to know a vintage by a whiff of its cork, now prefers baby food. Some days you just wish he would mobilize his roaring frustration in a single clear moment and off himself, then wish you hadn't wished it.

II
The leafless greybrown autumn
whispers ice up tree trunks,
making you want to head north
and plunge into winter like diving
into a cold lake. Taking it all
at once.

You think about hitching to Finland,
getting some cash and then throwing your wallet far
out the window as you cross the last bridge. How will you work
with no ID? Maybe you'll be the man with the golf cart who roams
around parks at dusk and picks up the trash. The park
and the dusk—you think that's okay. But while you heave the bags
you'll wonder if someone's left an unwritten letter
on the back of a napkin, something you should finish.

Your wife will spend evenings
prowling through the house looking
for what she exactly knows is not there,
a rift or a fault, settling finally
on the silverware drawer to look for blood
on the knife that cut something she cannot name or heal.
Your father-in-law will have forgotten already, will go on
eating oysters and outlive his wife.

I imagine you flinging your head like a retriever
shaking the nearly frozen water from his ruff,
looking at your watch, grasping the gate,
thinking about swinging on it like a child.
It is part of what holds you—the grids, the railings.
You give it a kick
and go indoors.

# The Chicago Picasso
*Chicago*

For over forty years, the sphinx of woman, dog, or bird
made of proven Cor-Ten steel that cloaks itself in rust
has prowled Daley Centre Plaza with its eyes—
two lenses in a single bound—no depth of field,
watching our paths speed up each year,
watching the startled hug of an accidental meeting
become thumb-jumbled text auto-corrected,
not too confusing, setting the appointed hour
and asking the perennial question: *I am here. Where are you?*
The 160-ton Picasso is always there, watching
hemlines crossing the plaza glide up and down,
ties flying in Chicago wind widened into gardens
of paisley and narrowed down to a black stroke. Every few years,
something goes dark: clothes, democracy, the honest
mystery of words. The Picasso oversees
the way we perform our cities: the organized hum
of Critical Mass, the earthy smell of farmers' markets,
the music that brings the world's songs into the Plaza.

The Chicago Picasso has worn
Cubs and White Sox hats and Blackhawks
helmets. It has become
rules about public art and witnessed
thought and force collide in the reflections
of courtroom windows.

Primeval, it has sniffed the air,
sussing out the alewives' die-off,
musk and catalytic converters in the Seventies,
then Chanel No. 5, Brut,
popcorn, the heated metal spoor of the El.

Through its lyre has whiffled
city impatience: honking horns,
shouts for buses, the thwack
of batons on heads and backs,
the hungry whine of the Loop.
It has vibrated with wind
the lake has stiffened with frost,
thrilled to the promises of a black president.
Puzzled as art, it suspiciously
sniffs the air while the garrison
of grids closes in.

# Rue Descartes
*Paris*

So the photographer, reasonable
statesman of the impossible, waits
for light and shadow to settle
with the stillness of gravity. Waits

for figure to conjure ground just
as Rubin's faces are about to kiss
across the vase that doesn't yet
hold flowers. Waits

for the warble of light
over the window to focus,
for each brick's turbulence
to grow still in the shadows.

The skeptical photographer,
believing in abstraction, doesn't
know she waits for something fickle,
the jazzman's mercurial change of key,

doesn't know that as she focuses she waits
for chance to become art.
Finding one equal music we send
something thrumming through it:

the murmur of sand in rumpled sheets,
a bicycle through a song.

# Acknowledgements
*by Kathleen Wall*

Veronica and I first shared our collaboration at a memorial gathering and reading for a colleague of mine, Dr. Kenneth Probert. Ken loved music and the visual arts almost as much as he loved the literature he taught, so this occasion seemed like a good venue to try out our experiment. Ken, like the entire Department of English at the University of Regina, was always a supportive presence in my creative life, and I thank both him and all the members of the Department for creating an environment that encouraged creative work as much as scholarship. I feel both lucky and privileged to have spent twenty-four years at the University of Regina's Department of English.

Paul Wilson, former editor of Hagios Press, attended Ken's memorial, and approached us afterwards to let us know that when our experiment grew to book size, he'd love to publish it. We both thank Paul for suggesting that a book of ekphrastic poetry was even possible; without his encouragement, this project would have stalled.

I began this project at a writers' retreat at Emma Lake organized by the Saskatchewan Writers' Guild. In this remarkable setting on a boreal lake, you can feel the presence of the Regina Five and even Clement Greenberg, who apparently visited from New York City—fascinated as he was by these Canadian Prairie artists. My conversations there with poets and visual artists mingled words and images together, urging this project along, and for that I am grateful.

This project was workshopped twice at Sage Hill Writing Experience. I want first to thank the volunteer board of Sage Hill for all the work they do to keep this remarkable institution running, and to credit Philip Adams, its Executive Director at the time of these workshops, for creating a caring environment that ran so smoothly that our muses never fled. Tara Dawn Solheim now keeps this extraordinary program running.

My first poetry colloquium was with the inimitable Don McKay. Who can sum up in a single paragraph the richness Don brings to a student's work? A man of wide-ranging ideas, he helped me construct the most useful paradigm for my work, while his attention to all the details of craftsmanship is unparalleled. Don brought his sharp editorial eye to the completed manuscript while continuing to teach me the poet's breviary of syntax, diction, sound—all married to idea. I am grateful to have benefitted from his deep understanding of poetry's resources and its significance, as well as for his guidance, generosity, and kindness.

My second poetry workshop was with Ken Babstock, who observed that I tend to stuff rather a lot into a poem, losing focus and effect. He taught me to trim with purpose and music in mind—to distinguish, in short, between a promising, interesting draft, and a well-crafted poem.

As well, I want to thank my classmates at Sage Hill—every one of them—for bringing such generosity and insight into our workshops: Madhur Anand, Kimmy Beach, Kimberly Fahner, Katia Grubisic, dee Hobsbawn-Smith, Margaret Hollingsworth, Dawn Kresan, Henry Rappaport, Angeline Schellenberg, Kevin Spence, Bernadette Wagner, and Kevin Wesaquate. I could not have hoped to find two groups of people more committed to poetry or more generous, insightful, yet challenging readers. Sage Hill not only brings wonderful faculty to Saskatchewan, it also gives writers an opportunity to be read by their peers.

A few of these poems were workshopped by my local poetry group, which at the time included Sheri Benning, Troni Grande, Tracy Hamon, Medrie Purdham, and Tara Dawn Solheim. This group, with their generous rigour, is one of the joys of my life.

I want to thank the University of Calgary Press for taking on our manuscript. A special thanks to Alison Cobra for her help with marketing, to Melina Cusano for her elegant work on the design of this book, and to Helen Hajnoczky, who generously shepherded Veronica and me through the publication process.

My deepest thanks are saved for my daughter, Veronica, whose photographs gave me an opportunity to enter a completely different poetic landscape, and whose attention to the surprises of urban beauty has changed the way I pay attention to the world around me. This collaboration has been an extraordinary gift.

# Notes
*by Kathleen Wall*

Several books and articles inform my reading of cityspace. These include:

Jane Jacobs' *The Death and Life of Great American Cities* (New York, NY: Random House, 1961).

Walter Benjamin's *Arcades Project* (Cambridge, MA: Harvard University Press, 1999).

Elaine Scarry's *On Beauty and Being Just* (Princeton, NJ: Princeton University Press, 2001).

Mark Kingwell's *Concrete Reveries: Consciousness and the City* (Toronto, ON: Penguin Canada, 2009)—particularly his notion of how cities give us an opportunity to try out identities, and his ideas about play in the city and the relationships between interiors and exteriors.

Gary Bridge and Sophie Watson's chapter, "City Imaginaries," and John Rennie Short's chapter, "Three Urban Discourses," both in *A Companion to the City*, edited by Gary Bridge and Sophie Watson (Hoboken, NJ: Wiley-Blackwell, 2002).

I first saw what would become the title of Section III of this book, "What Would Banksy Do?" scrawled on the side of a derelict building while driving on the TransCanada highway through Ernfold, Saskatchewan. I thank the anonymous artist.

Previous versions of the poems "First Snow" on page 75, and "Rue Descartes," on page 143, as well as their accompanying photographs, first appeared in issue #137 of *The New Quarterly: Canadian Writers and Writing*. Our thanks to the editors of this publication.

The epigraph found on page 31, at the beginning of Section II, "Questions in Our Pockets" is from a collection of posthumously published autobiographical essays by Virginia Woolf, entitled *Moments of Being* (London: Chatto and Windus, 1976), 72.

The epigraph found on page 65, at the beginning of Section III, "What Would Banksy Do?" is from Don DeLillo's novel *Underworld* (New York, NY: Simon & Schuster, 1997), 435.

The photograph on page 86 shows Anish Kapoor's *Cloud Gate* (2006, stainless steel sculpture, Millennium Park, Chicago).

The photograph on page 138 shows the sculpture by Pablo Picasso known as *The Chicago Picasso* (1967, Cor-Ten steel sculpture, Daley Plaza, Chicago).

# Biographies

KATHLEEN WALL is the author of two books of poetry, *Without Benefit of Words* and *Time's Body*, which won the John V. Hicks Long Manuscript Award from the Saskatchewan Writers' Guild. Her novel, *Blue Duets*, was shortlisted for the Saskatchewan Book Award for Fiction. She taught creative writing and nineteenth- and twentieth-century British Literature at the University of Regina for 24 years, winning the university's teaching award in 2001.

VERONICA GEMINDER is a photographer who works primarily in urban settings. Her focus is on capturing the beauty in cityscapes, whether that beauty has been created purposefully in public spaces, or accidentally in the boarded-over door off a back alley. She holds a Master's of Philosophy in the History and Philosophy of Architecture from the University of Cambridge.

## Brave & Brilliant Series
SERIES EDITOR:
Aritha van Herk, Professor, English, University of Calgary
ISSN 2371-7238 (Print) ISSN 2371-7246 (Online)

Brave & Brilliant encompasses fiction, poetry, and everything in between and beyond. Bold and lively, each with its own strong and unique voice, Brave & Brilliant books entertain and engage readers with fresh and energetic approaches to storytelling and verse, in print or through innovative digital publication.

No. 1 · **The Book of Sensations**
Sheri-D Wilson

No. 2 · **Throwing the Diamond Hitch**
Emily Ursuliak

No. 3 · **Fail Safe**
Nikki Sheppy

No. 4 · **Quarry**
Tanis Franco

No. 5 · **Visible Cities**
Kathleen Wall & Veronica Geminder

www.ingramcontent.com/pod-product-compliance
Lightning Source LLC
Chambersburg PA
CBHW042138160426
43200CB00020B/2976